BILSTON
IN OLD PHOTOGRAPHS

BILSTON
IN OLD PHOTOGRAPHS

—————————COLLECTED BY—————————
ELIZABETH A. REES

ALAN SUTTON
1988

Alan Sutton Publishing Limited
Brunswick Road · Gloucester

First published 1988

British Library Cataloguing in Publication Data

Bilston in old photographs.
1. West Midlands (Metropolitan County).
Wolverhampton, history
I. Rees, Elizabeth
942.4′91

ISBN 0 86299 515 9

Typesetting and origination by
Alan Sutton Publishing Limited.
Printed in Great Britain by
WBC Print Limited.

CONTENTS

INTRODUCTION

Bilston, part of the metropolitan borough of Wolverhampton since 1966, has a long history of its own. It is first mentioned in Anglo-Saxon times, in 994, when Wulfrun gave Bilston, along with other lands, to the monastery at Hampton which subsequently became known as Wulfrun's Hampton or Wolverhampton. It seems likely, however, that Bilston existed as a settlement well before this, although archaeological evidence is lacking.

By the time of the Domesday survey in 1086, Bilston itself belonged to the king while Ettingshall and Bradley were listed as the lands of William fitz Ansculf. The two hides of land in Bilston were worked by eight villeins and three bordars, which may indicate a total population of between 45 and 60. The value of the land had increased by half since pre-Conquest times. Ettingshall, however, was as large as Bilston again, while Bradley was half the area worked by four villeins. The total population of the Bilston area may therefore have been something between 100 and 150 compared with Wolverhampton's 150 to 200.

Bilston remained a royal manor until the reign of Henry III when the king granted the crown lands there to Walter de Bilston for his valour at the Battle of Evesham in 1265. Walter's descendants continued to serve the crown and they led the men of Bilston in Edward I's campaign against the Scots and on Edward III's expedition to France. In the fifteenth century they built themselves a large timbered house which is now the Greyhound and Punchbowl Inn, and which became the centre of their manor of Stowheath. Bradley remained a separate manor, held by the Pipe family.

In the course of the Middle Ages Bilston became a prosperous small market town and by the reign of Elizabeth there were nine families wealthy enough to have their own coats of arms resident there. Coal was mined from the fourteenth century onwards, some 5,000 tons a year being produced by the end of the seventeenth century, and other local industries were developing. Bilstonians became prominent outside the local area and one, Richard Pipe, became Lord Mayor of London in 1578.

Metal-working was well established by the eighteenth century and Bilston had become famous for its fine metal-work, buckles, trinkets, boxes and gun-locks. Revd Richard Ames recorded a mass of local information in his parish register, amongst it the names of more than a hundred bucklemakers and fifty chapemakers between 1716 and 1730. Most of these products were of cheap quality and were sent on to Wolverhampton and Birmingham for distribution to markets around the country.

At this time, Bilston also became particularly well known for its painted enamels which are much sought after today, especially the decorated snuff and patch boxes. These were made in small workshops, mainly by the family unit, although some larger manufacturers employed apprentices and other workers. One of the wealthiest families involved was that of the Bickleys and John Bickley, who died in 1776, was able to leave £1,000 to each of his children, as well as £40 each to two servants. The enamelling trade died out, however, as public taste changed and as such craft industries were overtaken by the development of industrial processes. Its successor was the mechanised japanning of tin-plate wares which continued well into the present century both in Bilston and in Wolverhampton.

The last quarter of the eighteenth century saw rapid industrialisation of the area. John Wilkinson established his ironworks at Bradley, canals were cut and increasing numbers of mines and foundries were started. More than 300,000 tons of coal were mined in 1827 and by 1860 there were 61 collieries in Bilston, employing 2,000 miners. The railway arrived in Bilston in 1849.

All this brought about a rapid increase in population, from 3,000 in 1780 to 7,000 in 1801 and 24,000 by 1851, leading to overcrowding, bad housing and insanitary conditions. Labourers moving from other parts of the country tended to congregate in particular streets, courts or yards which sometimes took their names from their inhabitants – local rural migrants in Shropshire Row, later called Salop Street, Scots in Caledonia Street and Irish in Shamrock Yard.

Such conditions gave an ideal breeding ground for the cholera epidemic of 1832 which killed one in twenty of the population of the town in seven weeks. The shock brought about some improvements in conditions, but it took a further epidemic in 1849 when another 600 people died to bring about real changes. A Local Board of Health was established in 1850 and became the Bilston Urban District Council in 1894.

These bodies were responsible for providing Bilston with all the amenities expected of a town of its size – a town hall, a library, a market hall, public baths, hospitals, a water supply, a sewage system, a fire brigade, parks, a cemetery and housing. Gas and electricity were also provided by private companies. In 1933 Bilston was incorporated as a Municipal Borough with Herbert Beach as the first mayor. Municipal independence was retained until 1966 when, in a general reorganisation of local government in South Staffordshire, Bilston was amalgamated with Wolverhampton.

During the early twentieth century Bilston became increasingly industrialised and the brochure for the 1933 Charter Ceremony mentions the manufacture of pig-iron, steel bars and strip, galvanised sheets, steel stampings and pressings, boilers, castings, bolts and nuts, tubes, aircraft components and hollow-ware amongst what it boasts are the hundred trades of Bilston. Most of these, however, were heavy industries, all interconnected and the town has suffered badly in periods of recession, first in the 1930s when it was included in Fenner Brockway's book *Hungry England*, and then again in more recent years.

The revival of heavy industry in the war and post-war years did not last and the establishment of newer industries has been largely insufficient to take up Bilston's surplus labour. The closure of the steelworks in 1979 was symbolic of the fortunes of the town as a whole.

The steelworks site is now the scene of redevelopment, with new houses and an industrial estate being built and open-cast mining in operation, albeit in the face of local opposition on environmental grounds.

In spite of its recent decline the photographs in this book will show that life in Bilston today is much better materially for the vast majority of people than at any time in the past. Pictures taken as recently as the 1950s show appalling housing conditions coexisting with a period of industrial prosperity, and it is a truism to say that the 'good old days' were by no means as good for everybody.

However, through all these changes Bilston has retained its individuality and something of its small-town character. All around there are physical reminders of the best as well as the worst of all the phases it has passed through.

The oldest building in the town is the Greyhound and Punchbowl Inn, a fine survival of the fifteenth century, but a great many of Bilston's eighteenth-century houses have escaped the developer and their elegant proportions still grace all the main streets, although many are hidden on the ground floor by modern shop-fronts.

The nineteenth century also added some fine public buildings to the townscape. The Town Hall, St Leonard's and St Mary's churches, as well as St Leonard's vicarage and many other private houses in the new streets radiating out from the town centre, all date from this period, as did the considerable number of nonconformist chapels, now mostly demolished.

The twentieth century's most significant contribution has probably been the construction of large estates of new houses to ease the overcrowding which still existed in the town centre. Bilston indeed was at the forefront of planning in the 1930s when it employed Charles Reilly to implement his 'village green' ideas, in the building of the Stowlawn estate in particular.

Bilston's history is reflected in the landscape of the town today and we are fortunate in possessing a large collection of photographs documenting life in the town over the past century, as well as buildings which have long-since disappeared. Of particular value are those taken by the local historian and raconteur John Freeman at the beginning of this century, the originals of which are preserved at Bilston Public Library. Many of the pictures in this collection are being published for the first time, together with many others from the holdings of both Bilston and Wolverhampton Public Libraries. Long-standing Bilstonians will enjoy looking back at scenes they may remember from their youth, while younger or more recent residents will see how their town has become what it is today.

High Street and Church Street

High Street, with its extension Church Street, is the main shopping thoroughfare of Bilston. Until the early nineteenth century it was also the main through road of the town, carrying the highway from Wolverhampton to Wednesbury which at that time ran along Wolverhampton Street and along High Street and Church Street to join Swan Bank. Although it has now lost that function the street is still generally crowded with traffic. Church Street was also the early market-place of Bilston so it was fitting that the Town Commissioners decided to build the Market Hall there in 1892. The market has now moved away from the main street, but access may still be gained to it from High Street.

In earlier times it was customary for the wealthier citizens of a town to build their houses on the main street and Bilston was no exception. The only one now standing is the Greyhound and Punchbowl Inn, former home of the de Bilston family, but a number of others also once stood on this street, including two believed to have belonged to different branches of the Perry family. The street was also well provided with places of entertainment – numerous inns and public houses, the original Bilston theatre in the Market Place and later a number of cinemas. Today only a few public houses remain and Bilston has no cinema or theatre of its own.

High Street and Church Street have undergone many changes over the centuries, but today the most obvious feature is the redevelopment of the late 1960s and early 1970s which demolished many of the old shops and the Market Hall. These were replaced with a modern shopping centre, including a new indoor and outdoor market. These continue to attract crowds from Bilston and elsewhere on market days, but unfortunately many of the other shops have closed in recent times so that the street no longer retains its once prosperous air. The photographs are a reminder of the numerous small businesses and places of entertainment that once typified High Street and Church Street.

THE GREYHOUND INN, High Street, before restoration. Originally part of the manor house of Stowheath, the Greyhound Inn was built c. 1450. It is known to have been lived in first by the de Bilstons, then by the Mollesleys and finally by the Green family until at least 1715 and probably longer. It became a public house in 1820 and over the years fell into a state of disrepair until the decision was taken to restore it in 1936.

THE INTERIOR OF THE GREYHOUND INN, pictured in 1936 shortly after restoration.

The Old "Greyhound" at Bilston, Staffs.

THE GREYHOUND INN, pictured in the 1950s. The Savoy Cinema, opened in 1927 and part of the empire of the Wood family, can also be seen. This cinema closed in 1962 and was demolished to make way for a supermarket.

THE SEVEN STARS INN, at the corner of High Street and Dudley Street, before and after rebuilding in 1934. The old building was part of a farm before it was converted into a pub.

HIGH STREET METHODIST CHURCH, pictured in about 1963. This church was built in 1841, closing and being demolished after its amalgamation with Swan Bank Church in 1962 to form the new Bilston Methodist Church. A drinking fountain which formerly stood outside was one of three presented to the town in 1866 by John Mason in memory of his wife Sarah.

LITTLE JOHN'S NEWSAGENTS SHOP in High Street. This shop stood next to the Turks Head public house and the board outside relating to the Kaiser's illness dates the photograph to c. 1910.

SHELLEY'S CHEMIST, High Street, pictured in 1941. The building is distinguished by the bust of Aesculapius, Roman god of medicine, which can still be seen although the shop is no longer a chemists.

THE BILSTON WORKHOUSE which stood off High Street in Workhouse Fold, the area which now lies between Smith Street and Hartshorne Street. The workhouse was built in 1737.

WORKHOUSE FOLD around the turn of the century.

MARSH'S BUTCHERS SHOP, High Street in 1955. The picture shows H. Thomas and staff.

THE ALHAMBRA CINEMA, High Street, pictured in the mid-1950s. This cinema was originally owned by Thomas Jackson of Wolverhampton, but eventually passed into the hands of the Wood family who operated it until 1927. It then went through a bewildering series of owners until the early 1960s when it was used to show Indian films and became Bilston's last surviving cinema. It has now been 'temporarily closed' for a number of years.

BUILDINGS IN HIGH STREET, formerly a school and later a furniture shop owned by the mother of Herbert Beach. She was not slow to support her son by displaying his election posters, promising town improvements, on her derelict property.

DELANY'S, ironmongers, Church Street.

CHURCH STREET, looking towards High Street, c. 1910. Harper's wines and spirits, also known as the Old Boars' Head, is marked by the sign of a genuine boar's head above the door. The large eighteenth-century house had once belonged to a Dr Bailey, but has long since been converted to shops.

THE OLD MARKET HALL, opened 9 August 1892 by Sir Alfred Hickman MP. The souvenir brochure commented that to Church Street 'the building is a welcome addition to the otherwise meagre architecture for which the street is noted.' It is believed to have been one of the first markets in England lit by electric light.

INTERIOR OF THE OLD MARKET. These were the open stalls provided for fruit and vegetables. Lock-up shops were also installed for other goods.

THE LAST DAY OF TRADING at the old Market Hall, in the early 1970s.

CHURCH STREET looking towards Swan Bank at about the time of the First World War. The Town Hall is seen on the left of the picture and the Electric Theatre/Grand Cinema on the right. This opened in around 1913 and lasted until 1921 when the luxurious new Woods Palace Cinema opened around the corner.

J FORRESTER, auctioneers, Church Street, 1921. This building was formerly the Grand Cinema and some details of its previous existence remain in the decorative doors, box office windows and gates.

THOMPSON'S 'OLD CHAINEY SHOP', Church Street, seen from the junction of Stafford Street.

TIMBERED HOUSE, Church Street, discovered in the course of demolition in the 1960s. It is thought to be part of a mansion belonging to the Perry family, dating from the sixteenth century and later converted to a public house called the Mitre. The remains were in a poor state of preservation and had to be demolished.

THE HOME AND COLONIAL STORES in Church Street, c. 1905.

J.E. DOWNS, butchers shop, Church Street, c. 1930. This business was founded in 1888 and was famous for its own brands of sausages and pork pies until it closed down in the 1960s.

WOOLRIDGE'S, Church Street, in the 1960s. The lady with her arm raised is Evelyn Smith, seen here with the rest of the staff.

DEMOLITION OF THE BOARD INN, Church Street, in October 1959. This pub was also known as the Hole in the Wall.

OLD BUILDINGS IN HIGH STREET around the turn of the century.

OLD GABLED HOUSES in Church Street. This building stood in the entrance from Church Street to the Pipe family house, known as Hell Entry, perhaps a corruption of 'Hall Entry'.

TURKS HEAD YARD, High Street. This was the last remaining dwelling house in the High Street, the name coming from the public house that formerly stood there.

Lichfield Street and Swan Bank

Lichfield Street and Swan Bank now form the main road through Bilston from Wolverhampton to Wednesbury. However, it was not always so. Wellington Road was constructed in the early part of the last century as the new turnpike road. Before that time the road from Wolverhampton ran along Wolverhampton Street, High Street and Church Street, before passing through Swan Bank to Bridge Street and on to Darlaston.

Swan Bank was known as the Broadway and was obviously a focal point of both the old and the new roads. Two coaching inns, the Fox and the Kings Arms, as well as the post office, were situated there. In later times trams and trolleybuses ran along this route and the tramways waiting room was also located in Swan Bank.

The two streets have also been at the heart of Bilston's municipal, spiritual and social life. The Kings Arms was used as a court room when the travelling justices came to town and also served as a lock-up for prisoners awaiting trial. In the 1870s the Town Hall was built opposite, at the corner of Swan Bank and Church Street. This later became the home of Bilston's first cinema shows and it was in Lichfield Street that T.R. Wood chose to build his new super-cinema, Woods Palace.

Both Swan Bank and Lichfield Street are adjacent to St Leonard's Church, the parish church of Bilston, but the name of Swan Bank is much more associated with Methodism. Swan Bank Methodist Church was the principal one in the town and its site is now occupied by the new Bilston Methodist Church. The old manse, however, still stands and the area opposite, which now contains the war memorial, is appropriately known as God's Acre.

Although much of these two streets has been altered over the years, a large number of buildings from the eighteenth and early nineteenth centuries remain either intact or above modern shop-fronts, and continue to distinguish one of Bilston's main thoroughfares.

SWAN BANK decorated for the coronation of Queen Elizabeth in June 1953.

BANK HOUSE, Swan Bank. Formerly the home of William Baldwin, a local ironmonger and ancestor of Stanley Baldwin, the Prime Minister, this house became the Dudley & West Bromwich Banking Company in 1866. The firm amalgamated with Barclays in 1916. The present banking hall, adjoining the house, was built after 1880 on the site of the old Swan Inn.

THE WOLVERHAMPTON STEAM LAUNDRY, Swan Bank, around the turn of the century.

THE TOWN HALL, built in 1872 and designed by Wolverhampton architect George Bidlake. As well as the public offices it originally housed the Bilston Free Library, established in 1870. It is now used primarily as area offices for Bilston.

THE CONSERVATIVE & UNIONIST CLUB, Lichfield Street. This building was formerly the Kings Arms, Bilston's principal coaching inn, and also the court of justice for Bilston and Sedgley. It was here that the murderer Abel Hill was first examined in 1819. It is said that he was placed on the balcony to watch the funeral of his victims, Mary Martin and the child she bore him, but remained unmoved. At election times the same balcony was used as the hustings.

THE KINGS ARMS BUILDING in more recent years.

ST LEONARD'S VICARAGE, built in 1820 and designed by Francis Goodwin, the same architect as the church itself. Revd William Leigh was the first vicar to occupy it and Revd John Ayling the last, in 1959. It has subsequently been used as offices and is currently undergoing restoration.

THE SWAN BANK TAVERN, known locally as the Blazing Stump, supposedly after a former landlord accidentally set fire to his wooden leg.

AN EIGHTEENTH-CENTURY HOUSE next to the Town Hall in Lichfield Street. Now the offices of solicitors Hall, Pratt & Pritchard, it was formerly the home of one of the founding partners, John Willim Hall.

THE TRAMWAYS WAITING ROOM, Lichfield Street, next to the Spread Eagle. The building was previously a gaol.

SWAN BANK METHODIST CHURCH, opened in 1823 to replace a chapel in Temple Street which had become too small for the congregation. In 1824 it became the first building in Bilston to be lit by gas, produced by its own plant. It was altered in 1840 and again in 1890 when it assumed its final appearance. After its demolition in the 1960s, the new Bilston Methodist Church was built on the site.

LICHFIELD STREET in the 1950s. The former Woods Palace Cinema had by this time become the Bilston Odeon.

WOODS PALACE CINEMA, Lichfield Street. The Wood family already owned various cinemas in Bilston and had long presented film shows in the Town Hall under the name of Woods Palace, but by the twenties they had decided to build from scratch a brand new picture palace. Woods Palace Cinema opened on 17 November 1921 with the film *The Old Nest*. On T.R. Wood's retirement in 1936 the cinema became first the Palace and then the Bilston Odeon which it remained until its closure in 1964. It has been a bingo hall since and the façade has recently been completely altered.

SWAN BANK in the early 1950s.

HEYNES STABLES, Bow Street, behind Swan Bank in 1954.

GETTING COAL IN THE MAIN STREET, Swan Bank in 1906. There were a number of small pits very close to the centre of Bilston well within living memory. This one was begun when excavations for a sewer uncovered large quantities of coal.

THE OLD LOCK-UP, Lichfield Street. The 'crib' was moved here from the Seven Stars Inn early in the nineteenth century. This building was later used as the tramways waiting room.

DIGGING COAL UNDER THE TOWN HALL in 1906. This was done because the building was threatened with subsidence.

SECTION THREE

Mount Pleasant

Mount Pleasant is the section of the road from Bilston to Willenhall which is nearest to Bilston town centre. It is not known how it got its name, but certainly in the last century it was a pleasant part of town. Some of the wealthier families such as the Bruetons had set up home there and its windmill gave it a semi-rural air.

It also had its industries, however, including Myatt's pottery and coalmines at Peascroft, just off the road. The town end of Mount Pleasant was also well provided with amenities, including the old-established Globe Inn, the Theatre Royal and the police station close at hand.

In this century Mount Pleasant has become more commercial and industrialised. As elsewhere in Bilston, fine eighteenth-century houses have acquired shop-fronts and private houses have been put to commercial uses, including the police club, now demolished, the Conservative Club and the Library, Museum and Art Gallery.

The firm of Bradley & Co, producing household goods under the anagram Beldray, set up their factory on a large tract of land on the left of Mount Pleasant, now given over to an industrial park. Here too was the Technical School, the tramways headquarters and the electricity company offices.

Mount Pleasant early in this century was therefore a hive of activity of all kinds. Today it is a busy road, providing the route to Willenhall and towards the M6 motorway, but it is still well used by pedestrians visiting the library, the annexe to Bilston Community College, the Citizens Advice Bureau or one of the numerous shops that still exist in the street.

MOUNT PLEASANT in the 1960s. A trolleybus turns out of the depot which was formerly the headquarters of the tramways company, while another negotiates the street towards Bilston.

THE GLOBE INN. Although this was a listed building it was demolished in the early seventies along with the police club, another listed building next door. The demolition of the club was said to have been an accident.

THE DRILL HALL in the 1920s. It was sold in 1968 and has been used as a night club since.

T.R. WOOD opening the new Library, Museum and Art Gallery at Brueton House on 18 March 1937. Mrs Wood stands on her husband's left, while the Mayor, Herbert Beach, is on his right. The Wood family lived next door to the library at what is now the Conservative Club. The coat of arms above the door is that of the Borough of Bilston, the motto being *Fidelitate et Industria Stat Bilstonia*.

BRUETON HOUSE, now the Bilston Library, Museum and Art Gallery. A house was originally built on this site in about 1818 by Thomas Brueton, a local manufacturer and philanthropist. His family lived there until the death of his widow, Sophia, in 1871 when the house passed to John Harper, a Willenhall industrialist who had married a niece of the Bruetons. On his death in 1903, his son Frederick inherited the old house and soon afterwards had it demolished and replaced with the present building.

Bottom right
THE POLICE STATION, after the damage caused by the riot of 21 July 1919. The trouble began with a fight between two soldiers and two policemen in Church Street which was quickly joined by a large crowd, who followed the policemen back to the station. Requests to send out one of the policemen were denied and the crowd began tearing down the wall outside and throwing stones at the building. Attempts were also made to burn down the front door, but these were unsuccessful and the riot was quelled at about 2 a.m. by the arrival of police reinforcements.

MOUNT PLEASANT in 1954. This house with its curious sundial stood next to the Technical College which can be seen in the background of the photograph.

THE THEATRE ROYAL in 1961, shortly before its demolition. Opened in 1902 as a variety theatre, it supplemented the live acts with films from about 1912 and became exclusively a cinema in the thirties. Reverting to variety in 1936, it thrived as part of the touring circuit under the management of Jack Riskit until his retirement in 1953, by which time the great age of live theatre was coming to an end. When its lease came up for renewal nobody wanted it and the theatre was eventually bought by the local authority and demolished. The site is still an open space.

THE INTERIOR OF THE THEATRE ROYAL in the late 1930s, after its return to live theatre.

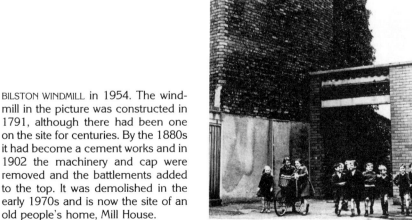

BILSTON WINDMILL in 1954. The wind-mill in the picture was constructed in 1791, although there had been one on the site for centuries. By the 1880s it had become a cement works and in 1902 the machinery and cap were removed and the battlements added to the top. It was demolished in the early 1970s and is now the site of an old people's home, Mill House.

THE TECHNICAL SCHOOL. Built in 1897 to commemorate Queen Victoria's Diamond Jubilee, it started with 80 students attending evening classes only. In 1949 the school became Bilston College of Further Education and was Staffordshire's first County College. It is now part of Bilston Community College.

SCIENCE LABORATORY at the Technical School. The building also accommodated an engineering room, a modelling and casting room, an art room, an antique room, examination hall and museum, as well as master's room and cloakroom.

SECTION FOUR

Oxford Street

Oxford Street was cut as the new turnpike road to Wednesbury in the 1820s, before which the main route lay along Brook Street. However, it did not remain an open road for long as it was transformed in the course of the nineteenth century into a densely populated area of courts, poor workers' cottages and small backyard factories.

Conditions in this area meant that it suffered greatly in the 1832 cholera epidemic, but it recovered later in the century to become a thriving local community with shops, pubs, churches and other amenities.

St Mary's was the first church to open in 1827, but it was followed by a United Methodist Church, a Congregational Church and a Catholic Church, all within about half a mile of each other. Today only St Mary's and Holy Trinity Catholic Church remain.

In recent years many of the shops and pubs, also becoming run-down and derelict, have gradually been demolished and the old terraced streets off Oxford Street have been replaced with modern housing. An industrial estate provides space for a number of factories as well as a night club.

Although no longer quite as populous as it was, the area around Oxford Street is still one of central Bilston's principal residential areas.

ST MARY'S CHURCH. The parish of St Mary's was founded in 1827 following a grant from the government to establish churches in the growing industrial areas of the north and midlands. The foundation stone was laid in November 1827 and the church finally consecrated in August 1830, having cost £9,000 to build. G.T. Lawley's *History of Bilston* attributes the church's mottled appearance to the porous nature of the stone 'which causes it to retain every particle of soot and dust that is blown against it from the chimneys of the works and furnaces around'.

SHOPS IN OXFORD STREET in the 1960s. The crossed shovels above the entrance gates indicate that this building must once have been a maltsters.

RAILWAY STREET, looking towards the Bilston Congregational Church in Oxford Street.

A HOUSE IN OXFORD STREET faced in the characteristic Bilston stone.

OXFORD STREET METHODIST CHURCH. According to the memorial stone this church opened in 1835 but no records survive before 1836. It closed just over a century later, in 1938, when the various branches of Methodism united and found themselves with too many churches. The congregation moved to Swan Bank and the building was subsequently demolished.

LEN HAYWARD'S MOTOR-CYCLE SHOP in Oxford Street in the 1950s. Many of the machines sold were still made in Wolverhampton.

SECTION FIVE

Around Bilston

ST LEONARD'S CHURCH, the parish church of Bilston, as rebuilt in 1826. A church is known to have stood on this site since the fourteenth century, but only the base of the old tower was incorporated into the new building, which cost just over £8,000. It was built in brick and did not achieve its present appearance until 1883 when it was encased in cement.

PIPE HALL, built in the eighteenth century as the residence of the last member of one of Bilston's most distinguished families, one of whom became Lord Mayor of London in 1578. The Pipe family's original house was in the vicinity of Hall Street and probably gave the street its name. Pipe Hall eventually became the Pipe Hall Academy, a private school, in the last century and is now a public house.

ST MARY'S VICARAGE, Bath Street, birthplace of Sir Henry Newbolt. This house was demolished in 1968 to make way for a sports centre run by former Wolves and England goalkeeper Bert Williams. It was perhaps an appropriate fate for the birthplace of the author of the famous 'Play up, and play the game'.

THE PLAQUE TO SIR HENRY NEWBOLT which was unveiled by the poet himself in 1927, the centenary of the building of St Mary's Church.

THE OLD SWIMMING BATHS, originally opened in 1853 and considerably improved in 1895, following their collapse in 1892. They were converted into a factory after the war and new baths were not built in Prouds Lane until the 1960s.

PINK POOL, off Prouds Lane. This cottage, lived in by Fan Taylor, was reputed to be the last thatched house in Bilston, while the Pink Pool itself was a relic of old mine floodings.

WALLETT & ROWLEY, fruit and potato merchants in Millfields Road, pictured in the 1920s. The building was originally part of the Ladymoor Tin School.

SHAMROCK YARD, named by the large numbers of Irish workers who flooded into the area in the boom years of the last century.

STONEFIELD MISSION, which began as a ragged school formed by Swan Bank Methodist Church in 1862 for the poor children of the area. Its first premises were a warehouse at an ironworks, but new buildings were erected in 1866. As the educational system developed, Stonefield became a mission church. When it closed in 1954, the £900 raised by the sale went to pay for the new church at Stowlawn.

STONEFIELD MISSION. The memorial stone was laid on 20 February 1866 by the widow of Charles Jackson who had originally founded the ragged school.

HALL PARK STREET in 1920. This was Bilston's first council-housing scheme under the legislation to build 'homes for heroes' after the First World War.

STAFFORD STREET. This house, faced in Bilston stone, is said to have been a bank and before that a school.

PIPES MEADOW, named after the Pipe family whose house, now the Pipe Hall Hotel, was in the vicinity. Sir Richard Pipe was Lord Mayor of London in 1578. The name, together with that of The Orchard nearby, is also a reminder of Bilston's rural character until the nineteenth century.

A MINER'S COTTAGE at Tenscore around the turn of the century. This was typical of many in the Bilston area.

ANOTHER MINER'S COTTAGE, this time in Ettingshall Road.

HAYMAKING in 1910 in a field now bounded by Cumberland Road, Birchdale, Rutland Crescent and Central Avenue. It was rented by the police and the photograph shows Sgt. G. Cartwright and constables W. Allman and J. Robinson standing on the ricks, with Supt. G.R. Pilliner holding the rake.

THE BILSTON CHILDREN'S HOLIDAY CAMP at the Bratch, Wombourne. The photographs show Walter Hughes, the mayor, and W.H. Pearson, head of Loxdale School, presumably with children from Loxdale. The camp was designed to give poor children a break in the countryside, but was closed in 1964 when it was decided that the buildings were beyond repair.

DANCING ROUND THE MAYPOLE at Etheridge School in 1953. The school had a long tradition of electing a May Queen and celebrating Mayday.

PICKING COAL AT PARKFIELDS probably during the coal strike of 1921. In times of hardship such activities were commonplace although, in the last century, they were heavily punished by magistrates who were often the owners of the coal.

THE BILSTON CHOLERA SCHOOL shown on a medal awarded to each of the original pupils. The cholera epidemic which was raging nationwide reached Bilston on 3 August 1832. The poor living conditions in the town gave it an ideal breeding ground and within seven weeks 742 people had died of the disease, 1 in 20 of the population. After the epidemic a national appeal was launched and £8,536 was subscribed to build a school in Fletcher Street, now part of Prouds Lane, for the 450 orphans left by the disease. At the opening of the school in 1833, each child wore its medal in a procession through the town.

PROUDS LANE in the early 1960s. The building in the photograph is the Bilston Cholera School, which by this time had become part of the japan works of Farmer & Chapman. It was demolished soon afterwards.

A WAGON OF THE BILSTON GAS LIGHT & COKE COMPANY at work on the lamps in Wellington Road, probably in the 1930s. The gasworks at Millfields opened in 1877.

WOOD STREET BAPTIST CHURCH, rebuilt in 1860. This chapel was originally founded in the eighteenth century as an Independent Chapel, but was closed, only to be refounded by the Baptists in 1799. The building pictured was demolished in 1972 and the congregation moved to their new church in Prouds Lane.

WOOD STREET and the Secularists Hall, where it is said that the Bible was once publicly burned. The building was later taken over by the Salvation Army.

HARE STREET, off Oxford Street, in the 1930s.

PINFOLD STREET photographed in August 1956. This house belonged to a Mrs Lambeth who refused to move and allow demolition of the street.

STONE STREET in 1934. These houses grouped around a courtyard were typical of many in Bilston. They were demolished soon afterwards.

WELLINGTON ROAD in the 1950s. The nineteenth-century houses in this road were of better quality.

RECONSTRUCTION OF THE BRIDGE carrying Wolverhampton Street over the railway line in August and September 1956.

GREENCROFT in the 1930s. This was another group of courtyard houses scheduled for demolition.

AN OLD TIMBERED HOUSE in Walsall Street, pictured around the turn of the century.

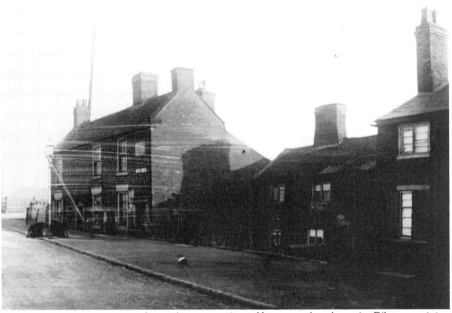

WOLVERHAMPTON STREET at about the same time. Here, as elsewhere in Bilston, mining subsidence meant that the houses were at many different levels.

STONEFIELD WALK in the 1930s.

PHILIP BATE'S GREENGROCERS SHOP in Bunkers Hill Lane. Minnie Rebecca Bate is pictured in front of the shop.

HARTSHORN STREET decorated for the coronation in 1953.

CHAPEL STREET. The plaque above the door is dated 1778 and dedicated to the Free Sober United Society as these houses were originally built by a trust. The society was dissolved in 1847 and the £590 raised by the sale of the houses was divided between the remaining 25 members.

BROAD LANES, Ladymoor. The entrances to the houses have sunk below the level of the pavement because of mining subsidence.

WAR DAMAGE, 20 August 1940. Because of wartime censorship the local paper did not say exactly where this bomb fell, but it destroyed one house out of a block of four, and killed and injured people in neighbouring houses. One boy was blown on to the roof of his home.

BILSTON WEST STATION in 1957. This station on the Oxford, Worcester & Wolverhampton Railway opened in 1854. Formerly known just as Bilston, it was renamed Bilston West in 1950 to avoid confusion with the Great Western Railway's Bilston station, renamed Bilston Central at the same time.

BILSTON CENTRAL STATION on the Great Western Railway, designed by Isambard Kingdom Brunel. Built in 1854, it was demolished in 1971.

COSELEY STREET. The pillared house on the left was the birthplace of Thomas Holcroft, the local engineer. From 1822 he was manager of W. & J. Sparrow's Bilston Ironworks and in 1878 founded the Bilston Foundry & Engineering Works, later known as Thomas Holcroft & Sons. The firm closed in 1969.

OPENING OF THE 2000TH COUNCIL HOUSE at 25 Park Road, Millfields, 18 March 1937. Pictured are Walter Hughes, J.T. Baker and W. Lofthouse, the architect.

THE KINDERGARTEN CLASS AT THE GIRLS' HIGH SCHOOL, Wellington Road c. 1930. The school was founded in 1919 at Brueton House, now the Bilston Library, Museum and Art Gallery, and remained there until it moved to purpose-built premises in 1930. The kindergarten was for both girls and boys, aged between five and nine. The Wellington Road premises later became the Bilston Sixth Form Centre and are now part of the Community College.

BILSTON CENTRAL SCHOOL opened in 1921. In 1947 it became the Bilston Boys' Grammar School and was replaced with new buildings in 1959.

TOLLHOUSE, Bunkers Hill. This stood at the corner of Willenhall Road and Bunkers Hill Lane.

TOLLHOUSE, Gibbet Lane. This tollgate at Stowheath on the boundary of Bilston is reputed to have been kept by William Perry, the champion pugilist known as the Tipton Slasher. This is the only one of Bilston's tollhouses that is still, at least in part, extant.

THE BILSTON WATERWORKS at the Bratch, Wombourne. They supplied the first water in 1896 and were officially opened by R.A. Harper in 1897. Wolverhampton Corporation took them over in 1959 and they eventually came under the control of the Severn Trent Water Authority. The pumping house was made redundant in 1986.

ST LUKE'S CHURCH was opened in 1852 and stood at the corner of Market Street and Pinfold Street. The church was originally built with a spire, but this was taken down to leave the stunted tower seen in the photograph. Having closed in the late sixties, the building was purchased by Wolverhampton Council in 1973 and demolished to facilitate the redevelopment of the area.

WOLVERHAMPTON ROAD flooded in June 1931.

TIPPING AT THE LUNT in April 1932. Refuse was used to infill the derelict land. The factory in the centre of the picture was a new one built on the reclaimed area, and the spire of St Martin's Church can be seen in the distance.

WARWICK STREET in the 1930s.

THE LUNT in the 1920s, before the start of reclamation work. Unemployed workers were taken on to improve the derelict industrial land for housing, allotments and sites for new factories.

FISHING IN THE CANAL at Bilston Steelworks, c. 1928. The men's wooden clogs, worn in the furnaces, lie discarded at their sides.

VILLIERS AVENUE, one of Bilston's newer developments, pictured in the 1930s. The Villiers Arms is on the left of the picture.

THE CANAL AT CAPPONFIELD in the 1920s. It is not certain what the picture depicts, but it is possibly an attempt to raise the boat which has clearly sunk. The building on the right is the Boat Inn and Highfields Bridge can be seen in the background.

HICKMAN PARK, opened in 1911 and covering 12½ acres of land donated to the town by the Hickman family. As well as the usual ornamental features, the park included an open-air theatre. This picture was taken in the 1920s and shows a cast-iron fountain of the type made at Coalbrookdale.

PLANTING A CORONATION FLOWERBED in Hickman Park in 1953.

PIPE HALL VAULTS, pictured in the 1950s. This was clearly a building of some antiquity, but nothing is known about its history.

A COURT IN TEMPLE STREET in the 1930s.

DERELICT LAND IN QUEEN STREET before reclamation. The football ground is at the top of the bank.

REAR OF HOUSES IN QUEEN STREET in the 1930s. Note the duck.

STOWLAWN undergoing reclamation in October 1945. German prisoners of war undertook the work.

STRAW YARD off Railway Street in the 1930s. This court appears to have been in a better state of repair than most of those surveyed by the council at that time.

HARROWBY ROAD celebrating the Queen's coronation with a street party, June 1953. After a tea of jelly and cakes the children were entertained by Mr William Shergold dressed as Old Mother Riley.

SECTION SIX

Bradley

Bradley has a distinct identity of its own, separate from that of Bilston, and indeed there have been recent proposals to remove it from the Borough of Wolverhampton and add it to either Sandwell or Dudley. As a village it is strongly identified with the Black Country and, in spite of many administrative and physical changes over the years, its sense of community remains.

The manor of Bradley was separate from that of Bilston, but it did not develop as a township in the same way as Bilston did. Much of the manor formed part of the hunting ground of the Lords of Dudley and, before 1700, there were few houses in the area. In the sixteenth century the Pipe family were briefly lords of the manor of Bradley, but they soon sold it to another local family named Hoo, and eventually it was purchased by the ironmaster John Wilkinson.

Since the eighteenth century, Bradley has been an industrial village. It is most famous as the site of John Wilkinson's first blast furnace, but even before that it was an important area for coalmining and a glassworks had been established in 1674. Wilkinson's works declined very quickly after his death, but the same advantages he had identified in Bradley – supplies of coal, ironstone, water and transport – encouraged numerous similar enterprises in the course of the nineteenth century.

Rapid industrialisation of what had been the smallest of settlements led to many of the same problems as at neighbouring Bilston. Quickly-built cottages for industrial workers were thrown up with little regard to sanitation and other amenities, and many of these buildings remained well into the present century. However, in the last 30 years whole streets have been cleared and rebuilt, and the pools and spoil heaps left by industrial workings have been redeveloped, either for housing land or as pleasant open spaces. Work on this had begun even before the war, when unemployed labour was used to make despoiled land into sites for new industry and parks and playgrounds.

Bradley was also very much a separate community in provision of shops, public houses, cinemas and places of worship, the latter in particular being especially plentiful. The six chapels and churches have since been reduced to two – a Methodist church and an Anglican – and residents now have to travel to Wolverhampton or Dudley to visit a cinema, but local shops and public houses remain, now serving new estates as well as the old village centre.

THE BLACK COUNTRY as shown in the *Illustrated London News* in 1866. The scene is actually the Fiery Holes area. Much later J.B. Priestley said of a similar view: 'This was the Black Country, unrolled before you like a smouldering carpet. You looked into an immense hollow of smoke and blurred buildings and factory chimneys.'

JOHN WILKINSON, founder of the first Black Country blast furnace at Bradley in around 1767. Wilkinson was one of the great figures of the early iron industry and was born in Cumberland in 1728. He moved first to Coalbrookdale in the 1740s, then to Bradley where there was an abundance of coal, limestone and iron ore. He died in 1808 and was buried in an iron coffin which he had had made for himself.

UNVEILING THE MEMORIAL TO JOHN WILKINSON, Great Bridge Playing Fields, 24 November 1956. Before this date the only reminder of the ironmaster remaining in the area was the cast-iron pulpit in Bradley Methodist Church. This plaque, also made of cast iron, was sponsored by the Bilston Historical Society and made in Bilston by John Thompson Ltd. It was unveiled by Amos Hunt of the Society and presented to the Mayor, Councillor W.H. Sandland, for the Borough of Bilston.

BRADLEY MINE in the last century. The first reference to coalmining in Bilston, from the thirteenth century, occurs in the manor of Bradley and the area was later famous for the 'Ten Yard Coal', a thick outcrop that could be easily and profitably worked.

WOMEN OF ST AIDAN'S MISSION, Daisy Bank, in 1924. The lady in the habit in the front row was Deaconess Grace and the mission itself was located at the back of the Britannia Inn.

SALOP STREET METHODIST CHURCH, opened in 1848 as a Primitive Methodist Church. It closed in 1955 and was demolished soon afterwards.

THE LAMB & FLAG, Salop Street. This public house was used as the Tommy Shop for Banks Bros.' Ironworks and was so notorious for fighting, both between men and between cocks and dogs, that it became known as the Hell House. Because part of the building was in Bilston and the other part in Coseley it was difficult for either set of parish officers to keep it under control. Ironically it became part of the St Leonard's Church property at the end of the last century, but was soon sold again in 1909.

THE OLD BRADLEY WESLEYAN CHAPEL, pictured in the 1890s. The first Bradley Methodist Chapel was the famous cast-iron one erected by John Wilkinson but, by the 1830s, this was inadequate and a new chapel was opened in July 1835, retaining the iron pulpit from the old one. It was enlarged in 1889 with the addition of the porch shown in the photograph, but in July 1901 it was struck by lightning and was too badly damaged to repair.

BRADLEY WESLEYAN CHURCH, Hall Green Street, built in 1902 to replace the old church struck by lightning the previous year. It was in use until the mid-1960s, when a steering committee was formed to bring together the remaining Methodist churches in Bradley. Recommendations were put forward to make the church smaller and warmer, but eventually it was decided to dispense with it altogether and Bradley Methodist Church now meets in the old Wesleyan Day School.

THE FIERY HOLES TOLLHOUSE, Bradley Lane. The memorial to John Wilkinson was erected on this site in the 1950s.

THE PRINCE OF WALES passing through Salop Street, Bradley, in 1927, on the opening of the Birmingham New Road. He was driven in a Wolverhampton-made Sunbeam car.

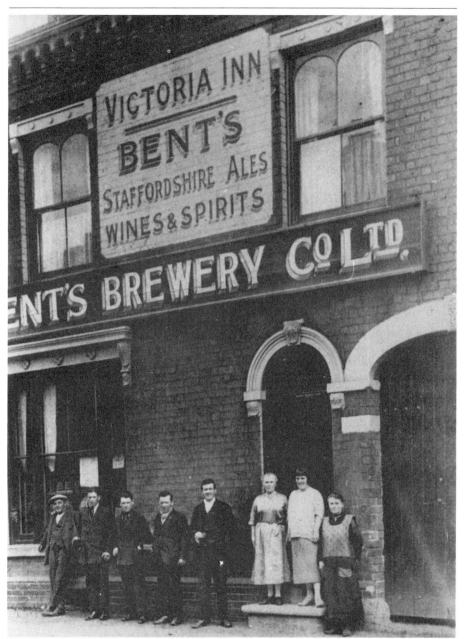

THE VICTORIA INN, Wesley Street, in 1928. Standing in the doorway are the licensee Mrs O'Brien, her daughter Lettice and her aunt Mrs Getting. The men are locals Jim Jeavons, Jim, Arthur and Tom Pearce, and Tommy Thompson. This pub, also known as the Stores, closed in the early sixties.

DAISY BANK STATION with Bradley schoolchildren leaving on a trip to Llandudno paid for by the J. Luther Greenway Trust, 25 May 1956. For many it was their first visit to the seaside.

THE FORUM CINEMA, Bradley, photographed as a bingo club in 1980. The original front entrance, replaced in the 1930s by the corner extension, can still be seen. This cinema, originally called the Queens Picture House, opened in 1921 and showed films until 1964.

WHATTON BROS. SHOP, Hall Green Street, pictured c. 1918. Mr Whatton, the owner, is on the left and the other man is Mr Hall who worked in the shop.

THE GREENWAY PLAYING FIELDS, presented to the town in September 1930 by J. Luther Greenway, the local industrialist. Unemployed workers were taken on to prepare the site.

CHILDREN AT THE GREENWAY PLAYING FIELDS in 1930.

HATTON STREET, Bradley, in 1955. This wash-house with its collapsed wall was shared by seven families who were understandably campaigning for rehousing at the time.

GREENWAY BROTHERS WORKS at Bradley, probably in the 1930s. The firm made galvanised iron sheets in Edward Street and also had a factory in Widnes, Lancashire. The owner, James Luther Greenway, lived at Tettenhall but took considerable philanthropic interest in Bradley.

CLEANING THE CANAL at Pothouse Bridge, Loxdale Street, probably c. 1910.

J. LUTHER GREENWAY receiving the Freedom of the Borough of Bilston, 21 July 1937. A director of Greenway Brothers Ltd., he was honoured for his local philanthropic work, in particular with local children. Greenway is at the centre of the picture flanked by the mayor and the town clerk.

SECTION SEVEN

Industrial Bilston

BILSTON STEELWORKS. Spring Vale Furnaces were purchased by Alfred Hickman in 1866 and operated as an ironworks until 1884 when he converted to steelmaking. By 1895 it was the largest integrated works in Staffordshire. However, after the First World War the plant was old-fashioned and in 1920 the works was sold to Stewart & Lloyd. It became part of British Steel on nationalisation and was closed in that corporation's rationalisation programme in 1979, in spite of strong local opposition.

JOHN FELLOWS' EMPLOYEES in 1911. This was a firm of stampers based in Temple Street. The youth sitting cross-legged in the front row, named Rogers, was killed at the Battle of Arras only seven years later.

THE PRIORFIELDS FURNACES of H.B. Whitehouse, pictured in 1912, shortly before the stack was demolished. The bricks were used to build houses in the Lanesfield area.

A DRAMATIC VIEW OF BILSTON STEELWORKS by night, showing the casting of pig-iron from No. 2 furnace in the 1920s.

BOILER EXPLOSION AT MILLFIELDS IRONWORKS, 15 April 1862, described by the *Wolverhampton Chronicle* as 'one of the most shocking and frightful boiler explosions that has ever occurred in South Staffordshire'. About eight tons of metal from the boiler rose 200 feet in the air, flew across the nearby railway line and into a field 300 yards away from the works. Here it buried itself five feet in the ground, having demolished three furnace chimneys in its flight. Twenty-seven men were killed in the accident.

A BILSTON PIT-HEAD early this century. This photograph was issued as a postcard with the comment 'On a wet day especially it cannot be said of the pit mounds "Earth has not anything to show more fair".'

DEEPFIELDS DRAINER, one of the pumping engines of the South Staffordshire Mines Drainage Commission. Flooding of the mine workings was a continuous problem in the Bilston area and one of the contributing factors to the eventual decline of the industry locally.

WORKERS AT JOHN THOMPSON'S ETTINGSHALL BOILERWORKS in 1870, about the time the firm transferred there. It was originally founded in 1840 at the Highfield Works, Bilston.

THE PIG BEDS at Bilston Steelworks in 1928.

A COALMINE in Moxley Road around the turn of the century. This very small type of operation was typical of the industry in Bilston where, for the most part, the terrain did not lend itself to large-scale working.

Bilston People

SIR ALFRED HICKMAN, born in 1830, son of a Tipton industrialist. In 1866 he purchased the Spring Vale Furnaces and turned them into one of the most successful operations in the midlands, in combination with his other coalmining and metalworking interests. He became an MP in 1885 and was also President of the British Iron Trade Association, as well as an advisor to the Board of Trade. He was knighted in 1891 and died in 1910.

BILSTON TOWN PRIZE BAND in 1932.

BILSTON POLICE FOOTBALL CLUB in 1920.

THE MEMORIAL TO JOHN ETHERIDGE at the Bilston Cemetery. Born in 1772, the son of a japan artist, John Etheridge lived in Church Street all his life. He kept a shop at his home and, as well as transacting his normal business, ran a savings bank and clothing club. He is also reputed to have given away 10,000 Bibles in his lifetime. His philanthropy was particularly evident during the cholera epidemics of 1832 and 1849 and he was made superintendent of the Cholera School set up for orphans of the first epidemic. He died in 1856 and 15,000 people are said to have followed his coffin to the cemetery. This memorial, detailing his life and work, was set up by the local people, but the soft sandstone weathered badly and it was taken down in 1948.

LIBERAL DEMONSTRATION, 20 June 1914, at Sankeys Field, Wellington Road, the crowd having been led in procession through the town by the Bilston Crown Prize Band. They were addressed by local Liberals and by Max Muspratt, the prospective Liberal candidate for South Wolverhampton, the constituency of which Bilston formed a part.

THOMAS REAY WOOD (1865–1938) was the son of 'Professor' Joseph Wood, a travelling showman who had skills in mesmerism, phrenology and palmistry. His early life was spent in the Isle of Man, when the show was not touring and it was there, as manager of the Grand Theatre in Douglas, that T.R. Wood met his future wife, pianist Zella Vondi, otherwise Nellie Hewitt from Handsworth. They settled in Bilston in 1910 and leased a number of cinemas in the town and elsewhere in the midlands. T.R. Wood also became an important figure in the civic life of Bilston, becoming chairman of the Urban District Council in 1925–7 and mayor in 1935. He retired from the cinema business in 1936 and died in 1938.

THE WOOD FAMILY, photographed at the back of their house in Willenshall Road, c. 1925. Standing are Thomas Reay Wood and his father 'Professor' Wood and seated are his son Reay, his wife Nellie and daughter Angela.

MRS BRUETON'S EIGHTIETH BIRTHDAY. Sophia Brueton was the wife of Thomas Brueton, a manufacturer and philanthropist and daughter of William Fletcher. Born in Mount Pleasant in 1780, she lived there all her life, at first supporting her parents and then, after her marriage in 1827, at Brueton House with her husband. Both were devout Methodists and her eightieth birthday was celebrated among her friends at Swan Bank Chapel. She died in 1871.

SIR HENRY NEWBOLT, the poet, one of the most famous people to come from Bilston. Son of the Revd F.H. Newbolt, vicar of St Mary's, Henry was born at the vicarage in Bath Street in 1862. His father died when he was four and the boy was actually brought up with his mother's family in Walsall. In his day, Newbolt was an eminent and also extremely popular poet, his most famous poem probably being 'Drake's Drum'. He died in 1938.

THE BILSTON CARNIVAL, 23 June 1956. The Carnival Queen was nineteen-year-old Margaret Harrison.

BEN BILBOE (1902–1951) as mayor of Bilston 1946–7. Secretary of the Bilston Branch of the National Unemployed Workers' Movement in the thirties, he stood for the newly formed Bilston Borough Council in 1933 and achieved the distinction of being elected while in gaol for a breach of the peace at a mass meeting the previous week. Much maligned as a communist by the local newspapers, Ben Bilboe continued throughout his short life to promote the cause of the unemployed and the poor in Bilston, and died well respected in the town.

THE CROWD AT BILSTON FOOTBALL CLUB in 1912. The number of spectators seems unusually large and may have been attending a cup tie or other important game.

EDWARD 'SCREW' WOOLLEY, owner of a screw-forging works at Spring Vale, was a well-known character in Bilston in the last century. He was apparently one of the last to wear the eighteenth-century costume of breeches, silk stockings and gaiters, never taking to the new fashion of long trousers. His firm, as was customary, issued its own notes and coinage with which to pay its workers, but Rushbrooke & Woolley's silver tokens were boycotted by the Wolverhampton tradesmen because, although the nominal value was a shilling, the metal value was actually only eightpence.

REVD CHARLES LEE, the last vicar of Bilston to be elected by the parishioners, in 1871. This custom arose from Bilston's historical status as a chantry rather than a parish. By the nineteenth century elections were accompanied by extreme acrimony and violence, and the custom was abolished by the sale of the advowson in 1880. Charles Lee died in 1909 and the next vicar was nominated by the Bishop of Lichfield.

VISIT OF PRINCE GEORGE, 24 April 1933, as part of a tour of occupational centres and Good Companions Clubs throughout south Staffordshire. At Bilston he visited the Loxdale reclamation scheme and the Lunt allotments for the unemployed, as well as the Laburnums Community Club. G.T. Lawley, the Bilston historian, then aged 88, was also presented to the prince.

BILSTON BOROUGH COUNCIL in 1933. Back row: Dr John Wells, J. Toole and J. Winyard; second row: G.H. Plant, J.E. Owens, J. Roberts, Mrs H. Holland, H. Homfray, J. T Baker, S. Hague and W. Leighton; front row: T.R. Wood, W.T. Fellows, Herbert Beach and W. M. Hughes.

BILSTON BOROUGH COUNCIL in 1963. Back row: Miss A. Fellows, Alderman O.H. Jones, Mervyn Williams (town clerk), Alderman N. Bayliss, G.A. Jones (mayor), E.W. Bold and R. Campbell; front row: J. Walton, G.C. Bold, J. Larkin, G.T. Rogers, T. Williams, E.H. Copeman, W. Pace, E. Beards, T.H. Larkin, G.H. Jones, H.A. Humphries, W. Fellows and A.E. Woolley.

WOOD STREET BAPTIST GIRLS' LIFE BRIGADE in the 1920s. Mr George Allcock, standing in the centre, was assistant and later church secretary from 1913 to 1936 and Miss Hilda Southwick, seated in front of him, was the first captain of the brigade and one of the first woman deacons of the church.

THE BILSTON FLOWER SHOW in the 1930s. This was one of the major events in the Midland social calendar for many years. Dr V.W. Lambah, at the centre of the picture next to Dr John Wells, was secretary of the flower show, as well as being Bilston's police surgeon. Also pictured are Mrs Lambah, who was Scottish although she usually wore Indian dress and Mr and Mrs T.R. Wood.

BILSTON ROTARY CLUB formed in 1931 and photographed at about that time. Familiar faces include the ubiquitous T.R. Wood at the centre of the photograph, Herbert Beach seated on his right, and Walter Hughes, seated on his left.

BATTERSBY'S PIERROTS in 1906. This troupe toured the Black Country, appearing at the many theatres which existed at that time.

THE BILSTON FLOWER SHOW, August 1951, the 62nd in the show's history. Pictured are the mayor and mayoress, Mr and Mrs E.W. Bold, Herbert Beach, the president of the Horticultural Society and Sir Lionel Smith-Gordon, the industrialist who opened the show.

THE BILSTON FIRE BRIGADE in 1894. Bilston's firemen were part-time, usually being employed on other duties by the Urban District Council. The ringing of the firebell in Market Street was the signal to drop everything and assemble for more important work. The horses also had other work until they were replaced in 1925 by the purchase of a motor fire engine.

HERBERT BEACH, Bilston's first mayor, in 1933.

J.V. LAVENDER, Mayor of Bilston, riding a merry-go-round at the Coronation Fair in Hickman Park, June 1953.

CHARTER DAY 1933. The Earl of Harrowby hands the charter confirming Bilston's new borough status to the first mayor, Herbert Beach. Mr and Mrs T.R. Wood look on.

THE CHARTER CEREMONY at Hickman Park.

ACKNOWLEDGEMENTS

Wolverhampton Public Libraries and the author are most grateful to everyone who has loaned or donated local photographs to their collections, either in the past or specially for this book. The author particularly acknowledges the help of the following in contributing pictures and information for *Bilston in Old Photographs*. Without their assistance the compilation of the book would have been impossible.

Mr D.H. Goodreid ● Mr & Mrs K. Woodroffe ● Mrs Angela Bird ● Ned Williams
Mr A.S. Wootton ● Mrs Bryan ● Mrs E. Smith ● *Wolverhampton Express & Star*
Bilston Historical Society ● *Birmingham Post & Mail*